THE WOMAN i DESIRE To be

What You Don't Desire, You Don't Deserve

JOSEPH A. SIJU

Order this book online at www.trafford.com
or email orders@trafford.com

Most Trafford titles are also available at major online book retailers.

Printed in the United States of America.

ISBN: 978-1-4907-1190-4 (sc)
ISBN: 978-1-4907-1189-8 (hc)
ISBN: 978-1-4907-1191-1 (e)

Library of Congress Control Number: 2013914650

Trafford rev. 03/17/2014

 www.trafford.com

North America & international
toll-free: 1 888 232 4444 (USA & Canada)
fax: 812 355 4082

Contents

DEDICATION

This book is Lovingly Dedicated to all the precious women in my life who have played a major role in my progress. Especially my Mother (Lady Evangelist Rachael Abegbe Fadojutimi) and my dear lovely wife (Mrs. Lolade Siju) and my wonderful daughter (Miss. Deborah Siju).

Acknowledgement

I want to glorify the almighty God of Heaven for inspiring the birth of 'THE WOMAN I DESIRE TO BE' This book is a result of my experience in conselling rooms and the observation of my mentors, Pastors Amos and Esther Fenwa. You are both indeed true and compassionate leaders.

My gratitude extends beyond the names listed below, to those who have supported my endeavors in so many ways; who have gone beyond the call of duty:

Pastor Toyin and Esther Adewumi of Christ Glory Ministry, Dublin Ireland. Minister John and Sade Siju, Sunday and Tomike Siju, and Pastor Tope Alex and Demola Siju who have a great passion for writing Christian literature.

I will love to appreciate Mr. Michael Emmanuel and Mr. Abiodun Aruna for their selfless work on the arrangement and the cover.

I celebrate all my pastor friends for their love and support for the birth of this book.

To all leaders and members of Holy Ghost Christian Center, New Jersey, whom God has used to shape my thinking and approach to ministry. You are the best congregation any pastor will love to lead.

Finally to my Family, my darling wife, Lolade Siju, thank you for your love and companionship over the past Eleven years. There is no better time to say I love you. To the stars in my life (Deborah, Michael and David Siju), daddy loves you dearly.

Foreword

This book is an epistle of requirements for any woman who wants to fulfil the divine purpose of God for her life. Many people do not really understand the reason why they were created to exist, it is like one's purpose explained in a script written before the act, knowing your personality and your make up can help you maximise your potential because an undiscovered potential is like a wasted potential, your eyes see, your nose smells, your ear hears; one must perform his /her role in life. It is not for only women, men can also read it to be able to know why the woman in their lives act the way they do, like I told a man your physical strength is to work more than your wife and to pay bills more than her especially as the husband and father over your home.

The woman I desire to be is for you to know your desire so that you can acquire what it takes to have a fulfilled purposeful personality.

Please take it, read it, digest and act it.

Amos Fenwa
G.O. HCC Worldwide

Introduction

The desire of a woman, this book refers to behaviors and characteristics of females within a religious tradition and also the influence that particular women have had on the growth of that tradition. Ignored for very long, women's desire is a topic that has attracted a great deal of controversy and interest since the arrival of the feminist movement in the past century. At the same time as early feminists criticized religions for legitimating patriarchy, later research has shown that as per religion, the desire of women varies considerably.

It has been said that human (Men & Women) beings are the only creation of God who never fully realize their potential. How tall will a tree grow? As tall as it possibly can. How fast will a cheetah run? As fast as its legs can carry it. How beautiful will a flower be? How loud will a lion roar? How sweetly will a bird sing? The majesty of the mountains, the grandeur of the ocean, the breath-taking beauty of the coral reef. The way of an eagle in the air, the fluttering of a butterfly's wings—all of God's creatures giving their best and fulfilling their lives

To evaluate women's desire, one must think about not only their place as being religious but also as a non-believer. One must distinguish between official teachings of religion and popular movements and between what is taught and what is actually practiced.

CHAPTER ONE

Who is a Woman?—The Makeup, Personality and Strength

Woman: Latest Version of God's Creation

At present, women put into effect formal leadership as teachers, preachers, ministers and even bishops in more or less every Christian denomination. However that is rather a recent development. As early as the seventeenth century, Quakers allowed women to preach, however majority of Christian groups did not allow women learn theology, to lead prayer, to preach, or to vote in church assemblies until the late nineteenth and early twentieth century. These exclusions were reinforced as churches accepted certain biblical passages that commanded women not to speak in church and on the notion that leadership in the early church was implemented more or less absolutely by men.

In the nineteenth century, a rush of religious passion, at least in the Western world, and a progressing movement for the suffrage of women both contributed to the augmentation of women's missionary movements. Women started to organize around offering housing, food, education, and a number of other social services for the deprived in their own homes as well as in mission fields in Africa, India, and China. Believing that women could do more than serve as quiet helpers to the men in the field, they also established educational programs to prepare women for the work of the missions.

Simultaneously, women started to seek an official voice in the churches. In the United States of America, Antoinette Brown Blackwell finished the theological seminary at Oberlin College in 1850. Although at first she was neither granted a degree nor ordained, she held a pastorate in the Congregational Church and was ordained in 1853. In November 1919, the International Association of Women Ministers, still an active group, gathered for the first time in St. Louis, Missouri. The Methodist General Conference declared women eligible to be licensed preachers in 1920, and in 1947, stated that women ministers should be accorded equal status with their male colleagues. Lutheran churches saw a movement in the 19th century to ordain women as deacons, but it was not until the 1970s that the American Lutheran Church and the Lutheran Church of America voted to ordain women as pastors. During the 1980s, the worldwide Anglican Communion carried on a lengthy discernment regarding the ordination of women. The Anglican Communion agreed in 1992 that ordination of women was approved but left an opening for individual dioceses to limit ordination to men, and at the time of this writing some Anglican and Episcopal dioceses still do so. A few denominations such as the Roman Catholic and the Orthodox still reserve ordination to men alone, although other administrative and teaching roles are open to women.

The women belonging to Christian Religion do not believe that gaining access to ordination and other official roles in the church means that women have achieved full equality. Ordained women still find themselves in smaller or more remote parishes or in assistant roles in larger places. Moreover, they find that Christian churches still need to pay more attention to women's voices as they develop Christian doctrine, morality, history, and spirituality.

Women were the first to proclaim that Jesus was raised from the dead. Women served as deaconesses in the first centuries of Christianity, lived as widows and virgins dedicated to lives of holiness as that lifestyle developed among those seeking to give themselves fully to Christ, and continued to reflect and write on the meaning of Christian faith and lifestyle throughout the Middle Ages. The 20th century, however, saw tremendous growth in the number of women engaging in professional theology, earning doctorates, teaching at the college and university level, and publishing theological works.

Christian women's theology is far from monolithic. Coming from different denominational and experiential perspectives, women theologians disagree with one another even on some fundamental questions.

One of the major theological tasks undertaken by Christian women has been to address the interpretation of scripture and what it says to and about women. Elizabeth Cady Stanton, in the second half of the 19th century, undertook to publish the Women's Bible, consisting of selected passages and commentary pointing out the patriarchal biases found both within the texts and in the church's traditional use of the texts. In the 20th century, women utilized a variety of scholarly tools now available to demonstrate that the inspired message of scripture can be distinguished from language, underlying assumptions, and customs that are reflected in but are not essential to the meaning of biblical passages. They also work to retrieve and reemphasize biblical messages that uphold the dignity of women and show their importance both in the history of Israel as God's people and in the early Christian community. In the last decade of the

20th century, Elizabeth Schüssler Fiorenza edited a history and an anthology of feminist commentary on scripture dedicated to the work of Cady Stanton and her colleagues.

One of the questions for women examining the Christian tradition has to do with the way in which Christians name and describe God. The importance of that question includes the fact that human persons are said to be made in God's own image. That being the case, does an overwhelmingly male image of God suggests that men are, in some way, more fully human than women? While most women acknowledge the special status of the name Father found throughout both Old and New Testaments and overwhelmingly in the teachings of Jesus, they point out that scripture also contains God's image that draws on motherhood as well as on the force and beauty of nature. They further point out that God is ultimately incomprehensible and cannot therefore be captured by a single name or image.

A number of women find the doctrine of the Trinity a rich source for feminine spirituality. Elizabeth Johnson and Catherine Mowry LaCugna point out that according to the tradition of Trinitarian Faith, God exists in eternal interpersonal relationship marked by mutuality and reciprocity. Thus, a Christian understanding of God bears witness against any human relationships or structures marked by domination or oppression.

One more key subject for women is the significance of the fact that Jesus of Nazareth, the revelation of God and savior of all, was a male person. Women theologians vary in their approach to this issue. Some suggest that the humanity rather than the gender of Jesus is the significant factor. Others search the accounts of Jesus's work to find examples of his equal regard for women and men. Some women like Mary Daly, who was a pioneer in Christian feminist theology, ultimately abandoned Christianity, concluding that with a Father God and a male savior, its message is inherently and irredeemably patriarchal.

Gen.2:18-23:

"And the Lord God said, it is not good that the man should be alone; I will make him an help meet for him. [19] And out of the ground the Lord God formed every beast of the field, and every fowl of the air; and brought them unto Adam to see what he would call them: and whatsoever Adam called every living creature, that was the name thereof. [20] And Adam gave names to all cattle, and to the fowl of the air, and to every beast of the field; but for Adam there was not found an help meet for him. [21] And the Lord God caused a deep sleep to fall upon Adam, and he slept: and he took one of his ribs, and closed up the flesh instead thereof; [22] And the rib, which the Lord God had taken from man, made he a woman, and brought her unto the man. [23] And Adam said this is now bone of my bones, and flesh of my flesh: she shall be called Woman, because she was taken out of Man."

Here is a quick question: What do you think would happen if you were offered an opportunity to pick one from these two options:

1. A 1996 model of Ford Explorer or
2. The 2013 model of a Ford Explorer SUV?

I am so sure that like me, almost everyone given this privilege will choose 'option 2'.

This decision is definitely based on very obvious reasons:

- The latter is more recent
- Will definitely be newer
- More adequately equipped technically
- Has more options and comfort
- More acceptable socially and
- More expensive and valuable to mention a few.

In this same light, when the Bible passage above comes to mind (Genesis 2:18-23) it seem clearer than the light of the day that "Woman" in creation was a product of an after-thought, improved reasoning and a move by God to solve a problem.

Everyone who understands this will know that the Woman was created to be a solution to an executive problem. Man, the crown of God's creation would begin to malfunction unless a solution was created to the problem of loneliness. When and if he malfunctions, the entire creation will be at risk. The Woman was created from the finished Man to be another of his kind, with solution to the problem discovered in man.

Please note that the Woman is Man (specie-wise), but a different model (newer model, most recent model) introduced into the system to be a solution to the problems of the earlier model. Just like The New Testament was introduced to amend The Old Testament. Hence, they both find relevance in each other. This is a basic and simple Biblical Truth that should not be misunderstood by anybody.

Basically from the Bible based explanations above, the following are inferred:

- The Woman is Man, and so has a life of her own
- The Woman is a Solution to the Problem of Lone-liness in man, hence has an assignment and a role.

1 Corinthians 11:7 KJV

"For a man indeed ought not to cover his head, forasmuch as he is the image and glory of God: but the woman is the glory of the man."

- The Woman is Different from man and should never Be placed in competition with man for any reason.—Both Man and Woman are created to relate based On roles assigned to them by the creator.

Temperaments and Nature

Men and Women share Temperaments almost at equal ratios but are naturally different physiologically, mentally and emotionally.

Temperaments

For the purpose of the subject under discussion, the human Temperament is a person's normal manner of thinking, behaving or reacting.

Human Behavioral Science recognizes two major divides namely:

The Introverts and the Extroverts

The Introvert:

Focuses primarily on his/her own mind, feelings and affairs, hence is mostly quiet and rarely social in nature.

Two basic temperaments were coined out of this nature:

- Phlegmatic—Not easily excited to action or passion, calm and sometimes quite sluggish. Not easily upset, tends to be attached more to nature than to people.
- Melancholy—Of a thoughtful and introspective nature, could often be affected with depression, a very deep thinker and is futuristic.

The Extrovert:

Is the opposite of an introvert. Is outgoing, sociable and highly concerned with outer affairs.

Two basic Temperaments were also birthed by this nature:

- Sanguine—Characterized by abundant optimism, anticipating the best, not despondent, confident, full of hope, a social animal, out spoken and talkative.
- Choleric—Very forceful, easily angered, goal getter, possibility thinker and very aggressive; could be very Unfeeling and tough. Action oriented.

As much as this literature is not about temperaments, it is important to note that both men and women are found in these classes. Most people (men and women alike,) blend different temperaments from these four sub classes, some even combining temperaments from the introvert and the extrovert classes.

Men and women all share this in common.

Nature

Naturally speaking, there are areas of life where there are clear differences between men and women. Some of such areas are as follows:

Physiology

The functions and activities of certain organs, tissues and cells of our bodies differ. There are even physical differences that are obvious to the eyes.

I will not need to delve into these as they are obvious; men are tough and rough, while women are tender and soft in general. Women carry organs aiding their role as mothers like a womb, mammary glands, female genitalia etc. While men have theirs differently made.

Mentality and Emotions

I do want to go straight to the point here, so I'll say men think more in terms of numbers, calculating their way through reasoning.

On the other hand, women are emotional beings, reasoning sentiments and third party considerations. While the man wants encouragement and a record of achievements and success because of his ego, the woman wants security, re-assurance and care. While the man is pursuing the practical figures, a guarantee will be okay for the woman. These and lots more you'll find in books meant for such subjects. I'll recommend some for you at the end of this work for further study.

Spiritually and Biblically

Spiritually, the Bible makes it clear that there's a air of equality between man and woman in spiritual things, but biblically, man is saddled with the responsibility of being the head in the home. This however is for the purpose of marriage. I hope it won't hurt you as a male reader if I directly tell you that you're the head of only the woman you married and not the head of every woman in town.

I Peter 3:7

"Likewise, ye husbands, dwell with them according to knowledge, giving honour unto the wife, as unto the weaker vessel, and as being heirs together of the grace of life; that your prayers be not hindered."

(". . . Heirs TOGETHER of the grace . . .)

I Corinthians 11:3;

"But I would have you know, that the head of every man is Christ; and the head of the woman is the man; and the head of Christ is God.

Ephesians 5:23, 24.

"For the husband is the head of the wife, even as Christ is the head of the church: and he is the savior of the body. [24] Therefore as the church is subject unto Christ, so let the wives be to their own husbands in everything."

These issues, as simple as they seem as caused so much trouble to mankind and the Church is not excluded. A lot of women, out of sheer ignorance of their proper identity have gotten involved in tussles with men over who is what when in the actual sense, men are not the same as women. There are no hierarchy issues except when it sometimes bothers on the home and marriage, even at this, a head is different from the neck and their duties vary and essential to each other.

I implore every woman reading this to stop every form of contention in the name of Women Liberation, or female equality with male. They are not necessary. Every man that's worth his salt knows the true value of a good woman, and every woman that is in touch with her identity and her maker knows that she is neither in bondage nor inferior to any man.

CHAPTER TWO

Our Case Study: Ruth, "The Woman I Desire To Be"

Ruth.1:1-21.

"Now it came to pass in the days when the judges ruled, that there was a famine in the land. And a certain man of Beth-lehem-judah went to sojourn in the country of Moab, he, and his wife, and his two sons. [2] And the name of the man was Elimelech, and the name of his wife Naomi, and the name of his two sons Mahlon and Chilion, Ephrathites of Beth-lehem-judah. They came into the country of Moab, and continued there. [3] And Elimelech Naomi's husband died; and she was left, and her two sons."

Despite the individuality of each and every one of us, our lives are entangled in each other's. We cannot safely dissociate ourselves from family decisions and it's consequences. The passage above is a clear case study; there was farmine in the land. Hence a MAN of Bethlehem of Judah went to sojourn in Moab WITH HIS wife and HIS two sons.

It so clearly seems that only one person had a say in the matter, he was the one travelling, others were an extension of his luggage.

Please take note that this tradition of silencing women and children was of Judaism and not about Christianity, hence the New Testament experienced the ministry of Priscilla and her likes. Some of the most experienced men in marital matters will agree with me that often when women are silenced, men fall into the trap of the enemy because her place is to solve the problem of man merely existing and being alone.

There's no other evidence from the scripture to instigate that Elimelech carried Naomi along in this decision or that he did not. Simply that the man took his family on a migration.

He wins the bread and so dictates the pace and place.

For Elimelech, the price was death. All men need to learn from this and a lesson for women who are covertly passive in the affairs of life. If you're passive, life will pass you by.

"And they took them wives of the women of Moab; the name of the one was Orpah, and the name of the other Ruth: and they dwelled there about ten years. [5] And Mahlon and Chilion died also both of them; and the woman was left of her two sons and her husband."

It would be of importance to take note of some hidden but vital spiritual truths in this story. This family is from among the people of God, blessed by God with an eternal inheritance of God's presence. They however made a wrong decision based on a temporal economic regression in the land without clarifying with God. They left BETHLEHEM for MOAB. Two interesting places. This man was of the tribe of Judah, Judah represents Praise, appreciated and satisfying. Bethlehem means a place or home of bread, a place rich in abundance of food, riches and established. The migration was to a land cursed by God.

Here is a short extract about Moab as quoted from Fausset's Bible Dictionary:

Moab"("from father"), i.e. the incestuous offspring of Lot's older daughter, near Zoar, S.E. of the Dead Sea (Genesis 19:37). Originally the Moabites dwelt due E. of the Dead Sea, from whence they expelled the Emims. Their territory was 40 miles long, 12 wide, the modern Belka or Kerak (Deuteronomy 2:10-11). Afterward, Sihon king of the Amorites drove them S. of the river Amon, now wady el Mojib (Numbers 21:13; Numbers 21:26-30; Judges 11:13; Judges 11:18), which thenceforward was their northern boundary. Israel was forbidden to meddle with them (Judges 11:9; Judges 11:19) on account of the tie of blood through Lot, Abraham's nephew, for Jehovah gave Ar unto the children of Lot, having dispossessed the giant Emims. It was only when Moab seduced Israel to idolatry and impurity (Numbers 25), and hired Balaam to curse them, that they were excluded from Jehovah's congregation to the tenth generation (Deuteronomy 23:3-4). Ammon was more roving than Moab and occupied the pastures to the N.E. outside the mountains. Moab was more settled in habits, and remained nearer the original seat Zoar. Its territory after the Amorite conquest was circumscribed, but well fortified by nature (Numbers 21:20, margin); called "the field of Moab" (Rth 1:1-63, and "the corner of Moab" (Numbers 24:17; Jeremiah 48:45). The country N. of Arnon, opposite Jericho reaching to Gilead, was more open; vast prairie-like plains broken by rocky prominences; "the land of Moab" (Deuteronomy 1:5; Deuteronomy 32:49). Besides there was the Arboth Moab, "plains (rather deep valley) of Moab," the dry sunken valley of Jordan (Numbers 22:1). Outside of the hills enclosing Moab proper on the S.E. are the uncultivated pastures called midbar, "wilderness," facing Moab (Numbers 21:11). Through it Israel advanced. The song (Exodus 15:15) at the Red Sea first mentions the nation, "trembling shall take hold upon . . . the mighty men of Moab."

Israel's request for a passage through Edom and Moab, and liberty to purchase bread and water, was refused (Judges 11:17; Numbers 20:14-21). In Israel's circuitous movement round the two kingdoms they at last, when it suited their own selfish ends and when they could not prevent Israel's movement, sold them bread and water (Deuteronomy 2:28-29; Deuteronomy 23:3-4). The exclusion of a Moabite from the congregation only forbade his naturalization, not his dwelling in Israel nor an Israelite marrying a Moabitess. Ruth married Naomi's son, but became a proselyte. The law of exclusion could have been written after David's time, whose great grandmother was a Moabitess. Israel was occupying the country N. of Arnon which Moab had just lost to Sihon, and which Israel in turn had possessed from him, and with its main force had descended from the upper level to the Shittim plains, the Arboth Moab, in the Jordan valley, when Balak, alarmed for his already diminished territory, induced the Midianite "elders" to join him and hired Balaam; virtually, though never actually, "warring against Israel" (Joshua 24:9; Judges 11:25).

The daughters of Moab, mentioned in Numbers 25:1, were those with whom Israel "began whoredom," but the main guilt was Midian's, and on Midian fell the vengeance (Numbers 25:16-18; Numbers 31:1-18). Moab's licentious rites furnished the occasion, but Midian was the active agent in corrupting the people. Balak (contrast, "the former king of Moab," Numbers 21:26) was probably not hereditary king but a Midianite; the Midianites taking advantage of Moab's weakness after Sihon's victories to impose a Midianite king. Zippor ("bird"), his father, reminds us of other Midianite names, Oreb "crow," Zeeb "wolf"; Sihon may have imposed him on Moab. The five "princes" or "kings" of Midian were vassal "dukes of Sihon dwelling in the country" (Joshua 13:21; Numbers 31:8). The licentiousness of the neighboring cities of the plain and Moab's origin accord with the more than common licentiousness attributed to Moab and Midian in Numbers 25. Eglon king of Moab, with Ammon and Amalek, smote Israel and occupied Jericho, but was slain by the Benjamite Ehud (Judges 3:12-30). (See EGLON.) Saul fought Moab successfully, himself also a Benjamite (1 Samuel 14:47). David moved away to Moab the land of his ancestry, fleeing from Saul, his and Moab's enemy, and committed to the king his father and mother (1 Samuel 22:3-4). Probably some act of perfidy of Moab, as the murder or treacherous delivering of his parents to Saul, caused David 20 years afterward to slay two thirds of the people, and make bondmen and tributaries of the rest (2 Samuel 8:2; in this war Benaiah slew two lion-like men, 2 Samuel 23:20; compare also Psalm 60:8, "Moab is my washpot"; yet among David's heroes was "Ithmah the Moabite," 1 Chronicles 11:22; 1 Chronicles 11:46), fulfilling Balaam's prophecy, Numbers 24:17; Numbers 24:19; "out of Jacob shall come he that shall destroy him that remaineth of Ar" (Hebrew, namely, of Moab). Among Solomon's foreign concubines were Moabitish women, to whose god Chemosh he built "a high place on the hill before (facing) Jerusalem" (1 Kings 11:1; 1 Kings 11:7; 1 Kings 11:33), where it remained until Josiah defiled it four centuries afterward (2 Kings 23:13).

At the severance of Israel from Judah Moab was under Israel, because the Jordan fords lay within Benjamin which in part adhered to the northern kingdom. At Ahab's death Mesh and Dibon, who had paid for the time the enormous tribute, 100,000; lambs and 100,000 rams with the wool, revolted (2 Kings 1:1; 2 Kings 3:4-5). (See MESH; DIBON.) His first, step was, he secured the cooperation of Ammon and others enumerated in Psalm 83:8-7, in an invasion of Judah, which was before Jehoshaphat's alliance with Ahaziah (2 Chronicles

20:1-35), therefore still earlier than the invasion of Moab by the confederate kings of Edom, Israel (Jehoram, Ahaziah's son), and Judah (2 Kings 3). (See JEHOSHAPHAT; JEHORAM; ELISHA; EDOM.) Mutual dissension, under God, destroyed this heterogeneous mass. Then followed the joint invasion of Moab by Jehoshaphat of Judah, Jehoram of Israel, and the king of Edom (2 Kings 3). The Septuagint states that the Moabite king assembled all old enough to bear a sword girdle. His mistaking the water glowing red with the morning sun for the mutually shed blood of the invaders (which observe he remembered had happened to his own and the allied forces attacking Jehoshaphat) caused Moab to rush forward for spoil, only to be slaughtered by the allies. At Kirhareseth or Kerak his immolation of his own son struck superstitious fear into the besiegers so that they retired (2 Kings 3:27; compare Micah 6:5-8); and then followed all the conquests which Mesha records on the Moabite stone.

Then too Moah, indignant at his former ally Edom having joined Israel against him, when Israel and Judah retired, burned the king of Edom alive, reducing his bones to lime; or, as Hebrew tradition represents, tore his body after death from the grave and burned it (Amos 2:1). Moabite marauding "bands" thenceforward at intervals invaded Israel, as under Jehoahaz (2 Kings 13:20). A century and a half later, in Isaiah's "burden of Moab" (Isaiah 15-16) Moab appears possessing places which it had held in the beginning N. of Arnon, and which had been vacated by Reuben's removal to Assyria (1 Chronicles 5:25-26). Compare also Jeremiah 48, a century later, about 600 B.C. Isaiah (Isaiah 16:14) foretells, "within three years, as the years of an hireling (who has a fixed term of engagement, so Moab's time of doom is fixed) . . . the glory of Moab shall be contemned." Fulfilled by Shalmaneser or Sargon, who destroyed Samaria and ravaged the whole E. of Jordan (725-723 B.C.).

As Ammon, so Moab probably, put itself under Judah's king, Uzziah's protection, to which Isaiah (Isaiah 16:1, "send ye the lamb (the customary tribute) to the ruler . . . unto . . . Zion") refers (2 Chronicles 26:8; 2 Samuel 8:2; 2 Kings 3:4). Moab contrasts with Ammon, Edom, Philistia, Amalek, Midian, as wealthy, abounding in vineyards, fruitful fields, and gardens, and civilized to a degree next Israel.

Hence flowed "pride (he is exceeding proud), loftiness, arrogance, and haughtiness of heart" (Jeremiah 48:26; Jeremiah 48:29; Isaiah 16:6-7). This sin is what brought on Moab destruction, "for he magnified himself against the Lord," boasting against God's people that whereas Israel was fallen Moab remained flourishing (James 5:6). In Isaiah 25:10-12 Moab is the representative of Israel's and the church's foes, especially antichrist, the last enemy. Jehovah, as a "swimmer," strikes out right and left, so shall smite the foe with rapidity, cleaving a way through them on every side. Zephaniah 2:8, "Moab . . . Ammon . . . reproached My people and magnified themselves against their border," i.e., haughtily seizing on the territory vacated by Gad and Reuben, E. of Jordan, after these had been carried captive, as if Ammon, instead of Judah, Israel's own brother, were Israel's heir (Jeremiah 49:1).

"Moab therefore shall be as Sodom (from whose doom her ancestor had been rescued) . . . nettles . . . salt pits (S. of the Dead Sea) . . . perpetual desolation." Moab was doomed to feel Nebuchadnezzar's heavy hand (Jeremiah 25:9-21), though for a time acting in concert with Chaldaean bands against Jehoiakim (2 Kings 24:2); but should recover after 70 years, at Babylon's fall, for righteous Lot's sake (Exodus 20:6). Spiritual blessings under Messiah are finally meant. Moab sent messengers to Jerusalem to Zedekiah (so read for "Jehoiakim") to consult as to shaking off Nebuchadnezzar's yoke (Jeremiah 27:1-8; Jeremiah 27:10-11). By submission to Nebuchadnezzar's yoke, according to Jeremiah's counsel, Moab though chastised was not carried captive as Judah. But for her usurpation of Israel's land, and for saying "Judah is like unto all the pagan," i.e. fares no better for having Jehovah for her God than the pagan who have idols, God "would open her side from the cities on her frontiers, the glory of the country (a glorious country in richness of soil), Bethjeshimoth, Baalmeon, and Kiriathaim, unto the men of the East," i.e. to the marauding Bedouin (Ezekiel 25:8-11). Sanballat of Horonaim, the molester of Nehemiah's work, was a Moabite (Nehemiah 2:19; Nehemiah 4:1; Nehemiah 6:1). Ruins in profusion abound in the country, betokening its former populousness and wealth. Their language was but a dialect of the Hebrew (which the Dibon stone proves, as also Ruth's intercourse with Naomi and David's with the Moabite king), as was to be expected from Lot's affinity to Abraham. Some of Judah's descendants in Shelah's line had dominion in Moab, and some Benjamite chiefswere born and settled in Moab (1 Chronicles 4:21-23; 1 Chronicles 8:8-10). The name of the family Pahath Moab, "governor of Moab," among those returned from Babylon (Ezra 2:6), implies a former connection with Moab as ruler.

Daniel (Daniel 11:41) foretells "Moab shall escape out of his (Antiochus Epiphanes') hand." So Porphyry says, in marching against Ptolemy, Antiochus turned out of his course to assail the Jews, but did not meddle with Moab, Edom, and Ammon. Nay, he used their help in crushing the Jews, Moab's old enemy; therefore Judas Maccabeus punished them with "a great overthrow" (1 Maccabees 4:61; 1 Maccabees 5:3, etc.). Isaiah (Isaiah 11:14) foretells the Jews "shall lay their hand upon Moab," i.e. shall occupy their land at Israel's final restoration.

It is amazing how a man with such richly blessed heritage will opt for doom.

"Then she arose with her daughters in law that she might return from the country of Moab: for she had heard in the country of Moab how that the Lord had visited his people in giving them bread."

Just after the total waste of the men, God visited Bethlehem (His people) with bread, abundance.

Flowers that bent towards the sun do so even on cloudy days. It wasn't long before bread returned to the place or home of bread. Dear reader, God is probably using this means to call you back home to Himself. There can't be lasting joy and satisfaction outside God. The world has only sorrow to offer, the noise and fun you see are temporal, and they are not the real thing. You might need to bow your head at this point and talk to God. Only in Him will you get to become the woman you desire to be.

"Wherefore she went forth out of the place where she was, and her two daughters in law with her; and they went on the way to return unto the land of Judah. [8] And Naomi said unto her two daughters in law, Go, return each to her mother's house: the Lord deal kindly with you, as ye have dealt with the dead, and with me. [9] The Lord grant you that ye may find rest, each of you in the house of her husband. Then she kissed them; and they lifted up their voice, and wept. [10] And they said unto her, surely we will return with thee unto thy people. [11] And Naomi said, Turn again, my daughters: why will ye go with me? are there yet any more sons in my womb, that they may be your husband's? [12] Turn again, my daughters, go your way; for I am too old to have a husband. If I should say, I have hope, if I should have a husband also to night, and should also bear sons; [13] would ye tarry for them till they were grown? would ye stay for them from having husbands? Nay, my daughters; for it grieved me much for your sakes that the hand of the Lord is gone out against me. [14] And they lifted up their voice, and wept again: and Orpah kissed her mother in law; but Ruth clave unto her. [15] And she said, Behold, thy sister in law is gone back unto her people, and unto her gods: return thou after thy sister in law. [16] And Ruth said, Intreat me not to leave thee, or to return from following after thee: for whither thou goest, I will go; and where thou lodgest, I will lodge: thy people shall be my people, and thy God my God: [17] Where thou diest, will I die, and there will I be buried: the Lord do so to me, and more also, if ought but death part thee and me. [18] When she saw that she was stedfastly minded to go with her, then she left speaking unto her. [19] So they two went until they came to Beth-lehem. And it came to pass, when they were come to Beth-lehem, that all the city was moved about them, and they said, Is this Naomi?"

Naomi now had to return home empty handed.

No husband, no sons and no grand children.

She however had a tough time sending her daughter's in law back to their parents. They simply refused to go back. Although after some persuasion, Orpah turned back, but Ruth remained unmoved by Naomi's cry and plea. Her mind was made up. She knew what she wanted to do and was not pretending at all.

Back Home in Bethlehem

"And she said unto them, Call me not Naomi, call me Mara: for the Almighty hath dealt very bitterly with me. [21] I went out full, and the Lord hath brought me home again empty: why then call ye me Naomi, seeing the Lord hath testified against me, and the Almighty hath afflicted me?"

Let's think for a moment. Who afflicted Naomi? Do you agree with Naomi that it was God that afflicted her? Do think her afflictions were self-inflicted, was tradition to be blamed or the idols of Moab?

Regardless of who is to be blamed, God was able to restore and He is ready to do the same for you.

Finally Naomi and Ruth returned to Bethlehem and it was the beginning of harvest.

Your return home is your beginning of harvest. All through the chapters of this book, you will find truths from the Word of God that will plunge you into a life of goodly harvests and fulfillment, becoming the woman God intended you to be.

CHAPTER THREE

Ruth Plus: Women and Relationships

Women generally are known to be relational beings. They keep deeply etched relationships. While a man by his make-up might easily jump from one bed to another based on the entrapment of his visibility. A woman's affection is heart seated and will not normally sell under frivolous circumstances.

The Holy Scriptures admonishes men and women on marital affairs, the Bible admonishes women to submit to their husbands, and men are admonished to LOVE their wives. The reason for this is not farfetched:

Women know how to LOVE as such love easily but need a lesson in submission, even though it seems very clear that women ought to submit, there seems to be a solemn practice of crafty control and domination deeply seated in their heart. Hence the Bible admonishes women to submit.

In African family settings, and most traditional family set-ups, the female child is believed to be more sympathetic and empathetic, more hospitable and caring; she never forgets her parents and siblings. The male child is often engrossed in the duties of winning the bread for his immediate family that he forgets others apart from his wife and children, especially when his personal economy is not very buoyant. On the other end, the girl child will still manage to smuggle something to her parents and siblings from her home no matter the austerity prevalent in her home.

This is a very strong point in the life of Ruth. She is an embodiment of selflessness all her life. She lived to serve the people in her life. It is often noticed that despite the attachment to her roots, a woman usually becomes attached to her husband and defends him by all means, covering his weaknesses and shame. Many times, even before being wedded to the man, many girls from richer and more comfortable homes give all excuses possible for the present state of their husband-to be, enumerating the positive expectations and brighter possibilities that will soon become reality. It is the hallmark of a good woman to possess such versatility to deeply love her parents and siblings, and also be very loving and protective of her husband.

As if this is all, then you will be shocked with admiration for a Ruth kind of woman when you discover her sacrificial and pampering love for her offspring. The love or dept of the relationship between a woman and her children is so mysterious that the Bible asked that "Can a woman forget her suckling child?" Well, the answer was to show the superiority of God's love for mankind, but it also tells us that the closest to it is the love of a mother to her child.

Several scriptures describe the love of God for His people as similar to the love a mother has for her children.

Although men also love their parents, siblings, wife and children, women are specially graced in this area. The Mother in a woman naturally rises up to the occasion to adopt everyone in need of love all around them, be it parents, in-laws, siblings, spouse, and their children, it is the reason, the life of a Godly woman is deeply rooted in sacrifice for others.

Ruth had a very good share of her relationships, first with Mahlon her husband, the son of Naomi, then with Orpah her fellow wife in the family of her husband, then with Naomi her mother in-law, culminating in her eventual relationship with Boaz her second husband and her son Obed.

Ruth plus Naomi

This is a very costly relationship, especially after the death of Mahlon (her husband). Ruth had no children and Naomi obviously old and seemingly hopeless without husband nor child. It should not be very difficult for any young woman of Ruth's age to do what Orpah did, hence the appreciation for the unusual sacrificial love Ruth showed to her mother in-law. This love was predicated on the love she had for Mahlon, which made her see herself as a replacement for him in the life of Naomi after his demise. The relationship of Ruth with Naomi was like seed sown, she soon reaped a bountiful harvest of it.

Ruth 1:8-22 KJV

"And Naomi said unto her two daughters in law, Go, return each to her mother's house: the Lord deal kindly with you, as ye have dealt with the dead, and with me. [9] The Lord grant you that ye may find rest, each of you in the house of her husband. Then she kissed them; and they lifted up their voice, and wept. [10] And they said unto her, surely we will return with thee unto thy people. [11] And Naomi said, Turn again, my daughters: why will ye go with me? are there yet any more sons in my womb, that they may be your husband? [12] Turn again, my daughters, go your way; for I am too old to have a husband. If I should say, I have hope, if I should have a husband also to night, and should also bear sons; [13] would ye tarry for them till they were grown? Would ye stay for them from having husbands? Nay, my daughters for it grieved me much for your sakes that the hand of the Lord is gone out against me. [14] And they lifted up their voice, and wept again: and Orpah kissed her mother in law; but Ruth clave unto her. [15] And she said, Behold, thy sister in law is gone back unto her people, and unto her gods: return thou after thy sister in law. [16] And Ruth said, Intreat me not to leave thee, or to return from following after thee: for whither thou goest, I will go; and where thou lodgest, I will lodge: thy people shall be my people, and thy God my God: [17] Where thou diest, will I die, and there will I be buried: the Lord do so to me, and more also, if ought but death part thee and me. [18] When she saw that she was steadfastly minded to go with her, then she left speaking unto her. [19] So they two went until they came to Beth-lehem. And it came to pass, when they were come to Beth-lehem, that all the city was moved about them, and they said, Is this Naomi? [20] And she said unto them, Call me not Naomi, call me Mara: for the Almighty hath dealt very bitterly with me. [21] I went out full, and the Lord hath brought me home again empty: why then call ye me Naomi, seeing the Lord hath testified against me, and the Almighty hath afflicted me? [22] So Naomi returned, and Ruth the Moabitess, her daughter in law, with her, which returned out of the country of Moab: and they came to Beth-lehem in the beginning of barley harvest."

Ruth 2:1-12 KJV

"And Naomi had a kinsman of her husband's, a mighty man of wealth, of the family of Elimelech; and his name was Boaz. [2] And Ruth the Moabitess said unto Naomi, Let me now go to the field, and glean ears of corn after him in whose sight I shall find grace. And she said unto her, Go, my daughter. [3] And she went, and came, and gleaned in the field after the reapers: and her hap was to light on a part of the field belonging unto Boaz, who was of the kindred of Elimelech. [4] And, behold, Boaz came from Beth-lehem, and said unto the reapers, The Lord be with you. And they answered him, The Lord bless thee. [5] Then said Boaz unto his servant that was set over the reapers, Whose damsel is this? [6] And the servant that was set over the reapers answered and said, It is the Moabitish damsel that came back with Naomi out of the country of Moab: [7] And she said, I pray you, let me glean and gather after the reapers among the sheaves: so she came, and hath continued even from the morning until now, that she tarried a little in the house. [8] Then said Boaz unto Ruth, Hearest thou not, my daughter? Go not to glean in another field, neither go from hence, but abide here fast by my maidens: [9] Let thine eyes be on the field that they do reap, and go thou after them: have I not charged the young men that they shall not touch thee? and when thou art athirst, go unto the vessels, and drink of that which the young men have drawn. [10] Then she fell on her face, and bowed herself to the ground, and said unto him, Why have I found grace in thine eyes, that thou shouldest take knowledge of me, seeing I am a stranger? [11] And Boaz answered and said unto her, It hath fully been shewed me, all that thou hast done unto thy mother in law since the death of thine husband: and how thou hast left thy father and thy mother, and the land of thy nativity, and art come unto a people which thou knewest not heretofore. [12] The Lord recompense thy work, and a full reward be given thee of the Lord God of Israel, under whose wings thou art come to trust."

Ruth had become the only thing left of all that Naomi had to rejoice over, her desires were all destroyed by death, husband and two sons dead, her joy, hope and right taken away from her. Many people like Naomi are living lives distorted, battered and wounded, while wallowing in their bitterness and anger, the only way to comfort is an unflinching love and care, selfless relationship offered them by the Ruths of this world. The woman you are today may be wounded beyond recognition, but there's hope for you if you seek refuge under the wings of the Almighty. He will give you joy and the sun will rise once again over your life.

Ruth plus Boaz
Ruth 2:13-15, 20-23 KJV

"Then she said, Let me find favor in thy sight, my lord; for that thou hast comforted me, and for that thou hast spoken friendly unto thine handmaid, though I be not like unto one of thine handmaidens. [14] And Boaz said unto her, At mealtime come thou hither, and eat of the bread, and dip thy morsel in the vinegar. And she sat beside the reapers: and he reached her parched corn, and she did eat, and was sufficed, and left. [15] And when she was risen up to glean, Boaz commanded his young men, saying, Let her glean even among the sheaves, and reproach her not: [20] And Naomi said unto her daughter in law, Blessed be he of the Lord, who hath not left off his kindness to the living and to the dead. And Naomi said unto her, the man is near of kin unto us, one of our next kinsmen. [21] And Ruth the Moabitess said, He said unto me also, Thou shalt keep fast by my young men, until they have ended all my harvest. [22] And Naomi said unto Ruth her daughter in law, It is good, my daughter, that thou go out with his maidens, that they meet thee not in any other field. [23] So she kept fast by the maidens of Boaz to glean unto the end of barley harvest and of wheat harvest; and dwelt with her mother in law."

Shortly after the natural flow of favor registered above in the quoted portion of the scriptures, Naomi intervened to help Ruth get what she deserved for her sacrificial love:

Ruth 3:1-4 KJV

"Then Naomi her mother in law said unto her, my daughter, shall I not seek rest for thee, that it may be well with thee? [2] And now is not Boaz of our kindred, with whose maidens thou wast? Behold, he winnoweth barley to night in the threshingfloor. [3] Wash thyself therefore, and anoint thee, and put thy raiment upon thee, and get thee down to the floor: but make not thyself known unto the man, until he shall have done eating and drinking. [4] And it shall be, when he lieth down, that thou shalt mark the place where he shall lie, and thou shalt go in, and uncover his feet, and lay thee down; and he will tell thee what thou shalt do."

Ruth 4:13-17, 21-22 KJV

"So Boaz took Ruth, and she was his wife: and when he went in unto her, the Lord gave her conception, and she bare a son. [14] And the women said unto Naomi, Blessed be the Lord, which hath not left thee this day without a kinsman, that his name may be famous in Israel. [15] And he shall be unto thee a restorer of thy life, and a nourisher of thine old age: for thy daughter in law, which loveth thee, which is better to thee than seven sons, hath born him. [16] And Naomi took the child, and laid it in her bosom, and became nurse unto it. [17] And the women her neighbors gave it a name, saying, there is a son born to Naomi; and they called his name Obed: he is the father of Jesse, the father of David. [21] And Salmon begat Boaz, and Boaz begat Obed, [22] And Obed begat Jesse, and Jesse begat David."

One good turn indeed deserves another. Love and truthful sacrificial relationship has turned agony into melody. As you decide to stand for what is right, loving when it really matters, God will put joy in your heart and give you the desires of your heart.

So what are you prepared to do to become the woman you desire to be?

Ruth Plus Naomi gave birth to Ruth Plus Boaz. This relationship in turn gave birth to Ruth Plus Obed. Obed is the father of Jesse, Jesse the father of David. One woman's desire brought her out of the bleakness of a cursed nation to the prominence of relationship with our Lord and Savior, Jesus Christ.

Dear reader, if you can pay the price, you will get the prize, and your reward might be far much more than you ever dreamt of. Let's go on to the next phase to see a very important aspect, showcasing the power of Desire.

 CHAPTER FOUR

Power of Desire

Psalm 145:16 KJV

“ Thou openest thine hand, and satisfiest the desire of every living thing.”

Proverbs 23:18 KJV

“For surely there is an end; and thine expectation shall not be cut off.”

Desire is a strong attraction towards something or someone. It connotes a heart sitted longing for something or someone. Although desire comes in different natures and degrees, it should be noted that desire is a very potent spiritual force, when applied correctly is a goal getter any day. A working desire is cooked up in a variety of necessary ingredients to make up a strong force that brings possibility to the fore in the life of anyone that possesses it.

The Bible passages above gives us important information about a desire from the Word of God. These cogent truths from scriptures are basis for the magnetic force field that powerfully surrounds the use of desire in our daily lives and in the pursuit of our destinies. God has respect for our desires and promises that what we expect will be given to us. However, a working knowledge of this vital ingredient for success as seen in the case study of Naomi and Ruth will give us a mind blowing boost to our faith. The extensive goodies hidden in the scriptures in regards to this Bible truth will further energize our faith life to stay on top of life's situations through the power of desire. It has been rightly said that desire is seated in the heart, a pointer to its operand effect over human destiny is noticed in the scripture below:

Proverbs 23:7 KJV

"For as he thinketh in his heart, so is he: Eat and drink, saith he to thee; but his heart is not with thee."

The Word of God here indicates that our lives move in the direction of our desires. Having said all these, it is of essence to note that desire can be thwarted and thereby delivering a negative result or failing to deliver any goods at all. The scriptures makes it clear through several pages that God is only interested in fulfilling our NEEDS and not our WANTS, especially our flimsy and selfish desires.

Psalm 145

"Thou openest thine hand, and satisfiest the desire of every living thing."

Other numerous portions of The Holy Writ outrightly denounces and nullifies the desires of the ungodly, the wicked, the transgressor, the sinners, etc

For example:

Psalm 140:8 KJV

"Grant not, O Lord, the desires of the wicked: further not his wicked device; lest they exalt themselves. Selah."
And

Psalm 112:10 KJV

"The wicked shall see it, and be grieved; he shall gnash with his teeth, and melt away: the desire of the wicked shall perish."

While the desires of the wicked perishes away, God's holy people are admonished thus:

Psalm 37:4 KJV

"Delight thyself also in the Lord; and he shall give thee the desires of thine heart."
When God is pleased with our desires, all that remains is to get the process right and wait for His deliverance.

Vision vs. Ambition

There are times in life, when vision and ambition are staged against each other because of the unhealthy pursuits we embark upon in our journey in life. Vision in this sense is a worthwhile goal we have pictured ahead of us, often received from God and it is not selfish. It serves as answer to the need of our generation, benefiting mankind as we get blessed fulfilling our purpose and assignment in life. Although, becoming ambitious about our vision could serve as a catalyst to its fulfillment, often too many people run after ambitions which are products of pursuing another person's goal, or in a bid to compete with other people. Often, such are usually very selfish, wicked and destructive. It seldom gives consideration to anyone else's welfare, it's conceited and evil.

When our desires flow from a Godly Vision and not from a selfish ambition, God places His supreme strength behind it to make it a reality, meanwhile, God sees to it that He frustrates the desires of the ungodly.

Consider this passage:

Isaiah 44:24-26 KJV

"Thus saith the Lord, thy redeemer, and He that formed thee from the womb, I am the Lord that maketh all things; that stretcheth forth the heavens alone; that spreadeth abroad the earth by myself; [25] That frustrateth the tokens of the liars, and maketh diviners mad; that turneth wise men backward, and maketh their knowledge foolish; [26] That confirmeth the word of his servant, and performeth the counsel of his messengers; that saith to Jerusalem, Thou shalt be inhabited; and to the cities of Judah, Ye shall be built, and I will raise up the decayed places thereof"

God practically makes it His business to inhibit the contemplation of the wicked.

Exodus 15:9-10 KJV

"The enemy said, I will pursue, I will overtake, I will divide the spoil; my lust shall be satisfied upon them; I will draw my sword, my hand shall destroy them. [10] Thou didst blow with thy wind, the sea covered them: they sank as lead in the mighty waters."

The desires of your enemies will not come to pass in Jesus name.

Desire and Disappointments
Ruth 1:1-5 KJV

Now it came to pass in the days when the judges ruled, that there was a famine in the land. And a certain man of Beth-lehem-judah went to sojourn in the country of Moab, he, and his wife, and his two sons. [2] And the name of the man was Elimelech, and the name of his wife Naomi, and the name of his two sons Mahlon and Chilion, Ephrathites of Beth-lehem-judah. And they came into the country of Moab, and continued there. [3] And Elimelech Naomi's husband died; and she was left, and her two sons. [4] And they took them wives of the women of Moab; the name of the one was Orpah, and the name of the other Ruth: and they dwelled there about ten years. [5] And Mahlon and Chilion died also both of them; and the woman was left of her two sons and her husband.

Death actually played a prominent role in dismantling the desires of Naomi. The death of her loved ones shattered her desires and made her a shadow of the woman she desired to be, losing her husband and her two sons in a strange land without any offspring for her sons was a blow too much for her to bare.

Death could actually be beyond just losing a loved one, Naomi was made irrelevant by her losses, her hopes dashed into pieces and taken away from her, her rights and her joy stolen away by the cold hands of untimely death.

For Naomi, life was not fair, if you are wondering whether it is just you and Naomi that shares these battered, distorted, wounded and bleak lives, and like Naomi, you are looking for whom to transfer your anger and bitterness to, just know that no one wants to share in your grief like Jesus does, and like He did for Naomi, there's a Ruth, waiting around the corner, she's God sent, an angel of light to lighten up the darkness in your life. She can only be found in Jesus.

Maybe you can sing with me here as The Holy Spirit fills your heart with grace and strength to do:

1. What a friend we have in Jesus, all our sins and griefs to bear!
What a privilege to carry everything to God in prayer!
O what peace we often forfeit,
O what needless pain we bear,
All because we do not carry
Everything to God in prayer.
2. Have we trials and temptations?
Is there trouble anywhere?
We should never be discouraged;
Take it to the Lord in prayer.
Can we find a friend so faithful?
Who will all our sorrows share?
Jesus knows our every weakness;
Take it to the Lord in prayer.
3. Are we weak and heavy laden,
Cumbered with a load of care?
Precious Savior, still our refuge;
Take it to the Lord in prayer.
Do thy friends despise, forsake thee?
Take it to the Lord in prayer!
In his arms he'll take and shield thee;
Thou wilt find a solace there.

A great lesson drawn from the story of Naomi is the truth that the problem is not the problem, but the real problem is how we see the problem. Too many children of God suffer and fight all alone because such people refuse to see their plight as an opportunity for God to show Himself mighty on their behalf. If you are in these shoes, God sent me to you to tell you that He's willing to help you, if only you can accept His help by stepping out of the ring and let Him be your tag team mate, not for you to live in denial, but to let Him, the master over every storm of life do what He does best, help you to calm the raging storm and stop the mouth of the enemy.

Decisions and Desperation
Ruth 1:6-19.

"Then she arose with her daughters in law, that she might return from the country of Moab: for she had heard in the country of Moab how that the Lord had visited his people in giving them bread . . . [8] And Naomi said unto her two daughters in law, Go, return each to her mother's house: the Lord deal kindly with you, as ye have dealt with the dead, and with me . . . [14] And they lifted up their voice, and wept again: and Orpah kissed her mother in law; but Ruth clave unto her. [15] And she said, Behold, thy sister in law is gone back unto her people, and unto her gods: return thou after thy sister in law. [16] And Ruth said, Intreat me not to leave thee, or to return from following after thee: for whither thou goest, I will go; and where thou lodgest, I will lodge: thy people shall be my people, and thy God my God: [17] Where thou diest, will I die, and there will I be buried: the Lord do so to me, and more also, if ought but death part thee and me. [18] When she saw that she was stedfastly minded to go with her, then she left speaking unto her. [19] So they two went until they came to Beth-lehem. And it came to pass, when they were come to Beth-lehem, that all the city was moved about them, and they said, Is this Naomi?"

Ruth, like a postage stamp glued to an envelop carrying precious a message, had made a vital decision to stick to Naomi, her mother-inlaw no matter what. Her desperation became known when she made it clear to Naomi that "Where you die I will die and where you're buried I will be buried . . ."

It is quite impressive to experience such a selfless determination. However, looking keenly at the scriptures through The Eyes of The Holy Spirit may give us a little more information on what informed Ruth's decision.

Naomi was about to return to BETH-LE-HEM, JUDAH, WHERE PEOPLE EAT BREAD AND LIVE IN PRAISES. (Moreover, there's news that God has visited His people back in Bethlehem with abundance of harvest). Her plea is for Orpah and Ruth to stay back in their CURSED, FAMINE-RIDDEN MOAB, WHERE IDOLS ARE WORSHIPPED.

Outside, sympathy and empathy for Naomi, Ruth had tasted the sweetness of serving Yahweh, (which by the way is not only measured in material goods and longevity, but spiritual peace and inner satisfaction) hence, returning to Bethlehem was not out of place.

Yet, kudos must be given to Ruth for the decision to probably sacrifice her ever getting married and getting offspring on the altar of her desire to become a Jewish woman, a child of The Most High God.

Ruth's desire to become an Hebrew woman or one of God's people landed her in fulfillment that was beyond her greatest desires. It must always be clear to us that the decisions we make that will benefit us on the long run may first be heavily sacrificial, causing us pain and denial of certain immediate gratification.

Desire and Delays
Proverbs 13:12 KJV

"Hope deferred maketh the heart sick: but when the desire cometh, it is a tree of life."

Some other women, whose stories adorn The Holy Bible would have tons of lessons to teach us on the subject of delay. Some of such women are the likes of:

- Sarah who had to wait endlessly for the conception and birth of Isaac.
- Hannah endured delay to become the mother of Prophet Samuel
- Rachael had to wait before Governor Joseph was born
- And Elizabeth the mother of John The Baptist.

Well, for Naomi to carry her first grandchild took a life time of waiting.

Losing to see her husband, her first son and her second son and a long painful and shameful journey back to Bethlehem—Judah. At the end of the day, was well worth the wait.

So, are you being delayed?

What are you waiting for?

Maybe it's simply your test and trying period or

God is waiting for you to come back home!

Whichever one it is, you need to learn very quickly that road blocks are not dead ends, the tests of life and the delays are not meant to make us bitter but to make us better.

This delay is there to proof the genuineness of your desire. How much do you really want what you claim to desire? It's time to rise and get it if you really want it.

Desire and Discouragement
Psalm 42:1-11 KJV

"As the hart panteth after the water brooks, so panteth my soul after thee, O God. [2] My soul thirsteth for God, for the living God: when shall I come and appear before God? [3] My tears have been my meat day and night, while they continually say unto me, Where is thy God? [4] When I remember these things, I pour out my soul in me: for I had gone with the multitude, I went with them to the house of God, with the voice of joy and praise, with a multitude that kept holyday. [5] Why art thou cast down, O my soul? and why art thou disquieted in me? hope thou in God: for I shall yet praise him for the help of his countenance. [6] O my God, my soul is cast down within me: therefore will I remember thee from the land of Jordan, and of the Hermonites, from the hill Mizar. [7] Deep calleth unto deep at the noise of thy waterspouts: all thy waves and thy billows are gone over me. [8] Yet the Lord will command his loving kindness in the daytime, and in the night his song shall be with me, and my prayer unto the God of my life. [9] I will say unto God my rock, Why hast thou forgotten me? why go I mourning because of the oppression of the enemy? [10] As with a sword in my bones, mine enemies reproach me; while they say daily unto me, Where is thy God? [11] Why art thou cast down, O my soul? and why art thou disquieted within me? hope thou in God: for I shall yet praise him, who is the health of my countenance, and my God."

Many times, we find discouragement in the places we expect to find encouragement. A very difficult and trying time for Ruth must have been when Naomi asked her to go back to her people. She also gave her very reasonable points. She's still young and had her entire life right in front of her, she'll need to re-marry and have children of her own.

Like I earlier stated, Ruth has tasted Jehovah and will not go back to idol worship, but when the person who introduced her to Yahweh now encourages her to go back or discourages her from going forward, it is very confusing and disheartening.

Her soul must have been cast down, hence her bitter cry.

Nonetheless, Ruth knew what she desired to become and so refused the enticing offer to cheaply bow out like Orpah did.

Today we find ourselves in countless discouraging situations, ranging from Spiritual leaders falling into sin, our model marriages breaking up and seemingly Godly homes ending in divorce. Then you might want to ask yourself if the walk is worth the work put into it. Just remember at such moments that, Jesus is our only perfect and worthwhile model.

Hebrews 12:1-3 KJV

Wherefore seeing we also are compassed about with so great a cloud of witnesses, let us lay aside every weight, and the sin which doth so easily beset us, and let us run with patience the race that is set before us,

[2] Looking unto Jesus the author and finisher of our faith; who for the joy that was set before him endured the cross, despising the shame, and is set down at the right hand of the throne of God.

[3] For consider him that endured such contradiction of sinners against himself, lest ye be wearied and faint in your minds.

Jesus is our only perfect example.

The Apostle Paul admonishes us to "Follow him AS HE FOLLOWED CHRIST." Meaning that when he's not living a life worthy of Christ-like emulation, then we should not follow him." (l Cor.11:1)

On your way to becoming the woman you desire to be, discouragement will come, but you can be sure that Christ will never disappoint you. People will disappoint you. Don't be too surprised or cast down in your heart when someone you expect so much from is flawed right before your eyes. We all have our flaws. Thank God Ruth refused to go back to her old life. When discouraging circumstances stares you in the face, remember to imitate Ruth: Simply refuse to go back.

Desire and Disgrace
Ruth 1:19-21 KJV

"So they two went until they came to Beth-lehem. And it came to pass, when they were come to Beth-lehem, that all the city was moved about them, and they said, Is this Naomi? [20] And she said unto them, Call me not Naomi, call me Mara: for the Almighty hath dealt very bitterly with me. [21] I went out full, and the Lord hath brought me home again empty: why then call ye me Naomi, seeing the Lord hath testified against me, and the Almighty hath afflicted me?"

Have you ever felt like hiding your head in shame or hoping that the earth will open and just swallow you to conceal your shame and save you from disgrace? If you've been through such path or you're actually there right now, then I welcome you to a new subject in the school of life, I call this 'DESTINY 106'. Six is the number of man, in all our frail frame, at best we are prone to silly mistakes, and some of the biggest errors come to keep us humble and keep our feet on the ground just before God shows Himself as mighty on our behalf.

Many times, it is not borne out of human error, but divine flooring that will keep us humble when we get to the great heights God is taking us to.

Some disgraces are fore runners of greatness, to give our glory a story to accompany it. No story, no glory.

So, Naomi returned totally empty.

At times things turn out in such a way that it seems the enemy's vows are being fulfilled. It seems they got their way, like evil triumphed over good. They are usually very sad moments; at times some people really give the enemy all the pleasure by committing suicide. Don't give up or quit. Those who cannot handle shame cannot handle stardom. On the stairway to stardom lies the pitfalls of shame, but they are not meant to stop you but are meant to toughen you up.

In the words of Ziegler, "When the going gets tough, the Tough gets going." "Quitters don't win and Winners don't quit".

Handling the season of defeat, which for God's children are temporal, requires quietness before people and praises in anticipation of a great change before God. The devil toys with our hearts at this point, manipulating us to blame God, he told Job through his wife to curse God and die. Thank God Job understood that it was a statement of foolishness. Hence, he praised God and waited till change came. Wait till your change comes.

This delay is there to proof the genuineness of your desire. How much do you really want what you claim to desire? It's time to rise and get it if you really want it.

Job 14:13-14 KJV

"O that thou wouldest hide me in the grave, that thou wouldest keep me secret, until thy wrath be past, that thou wouldest appoint me a set time, and remember me! [14] If a man dies, shall he live again? All the days of my appointed time will I wait, till my change come. Glory be to God, Job's change eventually came, he bounced back, up higher than ever, seven times over. WOW! There's some good news coming your way right now. This trial will now pass and the story is done. All that's left is the manifestation of your glory.

Isaiah 61:7 KJV

"For your shame ye shall have double; and for confusion they shall rejoice in their portion: therefore in their land they shall possess the double: everlasting joy shall be unto them."

Oh, maybe you need to pick up your Bible and read from the very 1st verse of the Bible passage above . . .

Verse 3:

"To appoint unto them that mourn in Zion, to give unto them beauty for ashes, the oil of joy for mourning, the garment of praise for the spirit of heaviness; that they might be called trees of righteousness, the planting of the Lord, that he might be glorified".

I dare to announce to you by The Spirit of Jehovah that it is your season of recovery already. Every shame goes out the window; your fame is knocking at the door.

Dear Woman of God, Daughter of Zion, or whoever you are under the function of this literature ministration, where you find DESIRE AND DISGRACE YOU'LL ALSO FIND "Desire" and "The Grace".

In the Bible Book of Luke, chapter number five, Simon Peter and his fishing crew Toiled all night but there was no result, nothing to show for it. The market women must have taken words back to the market place that Simon & Co. caught nothing all night. But just before the shameful news could spread long enough, The Master over every Storm stepped into Peter's boat. I am sure that the same people who carried the story would now spread the glory!

Peter had a net Breaking fishing expenditure. Your breakthrough is now.

Desire and Divinity
Romans 8:31 KJV

"What shall we then say to these things? If God be for us, who can be against us?"

When Desire is fired by Divinity, every enemy and setbacks are temporal. A Godly desire has its strength in tenacity and long suffering. Long suffering is not same with suffering long, suffering long is dying in the suffering, long suffering is waiting on God like Job did, it is enduring all night till Jesus enters your boat like Peter did, it is calling on Jesus to calm the storms as the disciples did. It is enduring the story because of the glory like Jesus did: **Hebrews 12:2 KJV**

"Looking unto Jesus the author and finisher of our faith; who for the joy that was set before him endured the cross, despising the shame, and is set down at the right hand of the throne of God."

The woman you desire to be would make you focus on the prize and not the price.

You should know the price and be prepared to pay it, but your gaze must be on the prize, that is "The Woman You Desire to Be". Swimmers cut the splashes, only divers get the pearls. You cannot kill a shark in the pond behind your house; you must go out to the sea.

As I round up this chapter, I will be opening up to you in clear terms, what it takes to become The Woman you Desire to be.

If you have read all through to this point, Grace is already upon you to take what belongs to you and become who you desire to be.

CHAPTER FIVE

Nurturing Your Desire and Vision

The beauty about "desire" is that from the moment it is conceived to the time of actualization is a process; a process that is dictated by time. It will be completely unrealistic to think that one could desire something this very moment and achieve it this very moment as well. It must be recognized that a series of events must take place in order for your desire to become a reality.

This can be likened unto a woman that is expectant with child. There is a time the child is conceived, after which a series of events occur before the child is actually born; the same is true for your desire.

Step One: Seed of your desire is planted in your heart (child conceived in the womb)

It is important for you to know that you must first recognize what you want. What are you truly seeking after? Take a minute to ask yourself this question.

Do you know what you want, what your dreams and aspirations are? Are you convinced that what you desire is what you really want?

Step Two: Seed needs nourishment (First Trimester with child)

At this stage in the pregnant woman the child is being fed with all kinds of nourishment thereby resulting in growth. Here the vital organs are growing and developing (brain, heart, lungs, etc)

Once you have recognized your desire, you must feed it with your passion (Your passion is the reason you wake up in the morning, and just the thought of it can keep you up late with excitement. But not everyone knows exactly what his/her passion is right away), your drive to see it grow, mature and become a reality. This in itself cannot happen unless you understand why you want what you desire. What is the root, the rhyme, the reason behind what you desire? Do you want it because other people have it? Do you want it in order to show off? Do you want it in order to be spiteful? You must recognize the reason for your dreams because your reason is what fuels your drive and your drive is what feeds your desire.

During this stage, you must do a cost analysis. What is the price for the materialization of your desire? You must know what sacrifices you will need to make. You cannot afford to go into it blindly, believing that "what will be will be". That's a false ideology; with the help of God you can create your own reality. Remember, "Nothing good comes cheap".

Lastly in this stage, your desire must have a depth. How badly do you want it? Do you want it bad enough that you are willing to pay the price for it? The reason I say this is because if you do not want it badly enough, it becomes very easy to abandon your desire without seeing its fulfillment.

Step Three: Seed begins to grow in visible ways (Second/Third Trimester with child)

At this stage everyone around the pregnant woman knows she is pregnant. There is a baby bump (the child is growing in size). During this time, there will be some physical steps you need to begin to take; you translate your desire from a dream in your heart to actual physical steps that will get you closer to your goal.

Please don't just sit and dream, you must work out your dream. Research what is needed to get you to where you desire and begin to take active steps towards it. Do you need to return back to school? Do you need to put your home in order? Do you need to begin that business? Make that investment? Whatever you need to do to make your desire your reality, start doing them today.

1st Thessalonians 5:17
Pray without ceasing (KJV)

As the seed of your desire grows, don't stop nourishing it. You must continually feed it with God's word/promises. You must continue to fast and pray about the fulfillment and manifestation of it.

Step Four: Stay with it (Time of Labor)
Here, the pregnant woman must go through labor, she experiences pain and challenges in her body to birth the child to life.

Job 14:14
If a man die, shall he live *again*? all the days of my appointed time will I wait, till my change come.

I want to tell you that many a time when its time for the manifestation of your desire there will be distractions, pain, hardships and trials but you must decide not to give up or give in. You must press forward until your change comes, Just like Job prayed.

So when you feel like you see the light at the end of the tunnel but the light is not coming quick or easy enough, remember you are in labor: Stay with it and your desire will be delivered in Jesus mighty name. Amen.

How To Develop Your Desire

Once you have identified your desire, here are practical steps needed for its development.

1. Write it down

    Habakukk 2:2.
    And the LORD answered me, and said, Write the vision, and make it plain upon tables, so he may run that reads it (KJV)

    Make sure you understand it and that others can understand it as well

2. Commit it to the hands of the Lord

    Proverbs 3:6
    In all your ways acknowledge Him, And He shall direct[a] your paths (NKJV)

3. Set measurable practical goals that will lead to the fulfillment of your desire

4. Pursue after it with the whole of your heart, don't give up, don't be discouraged

5. Celebrate every level of accomplishment, no matter how small.

    Zachariah 4:10
    Do not despise these small beginnings, for the LORD rejoices to see the work begin, to see the plumb line in Zerubbabel's hand." (NLT)

    As you do this, you feel encouraged to press on, you feel like you are making progress.

6. Shun all distractions. You must never allow anything or anyone distract you from your goals, your dreams and your desire.

Your Vision and Your desire

It is my conviction that a lack of vision is one of the sore points of every individual with an unfulfilled desire. Through my interaction with many individuals as a pastor, I have discovered that vision is central to making a positive and lasting impact in the world.

I am equally persuaded that until individuals exercise their abilities to discern God's vision for their lives and make wholehearted commitments to such vision, they will continue to struggle, live small, be sick and be stagnant.

Until our lives are vision-driven our desire and progress will be put in abeyance

1. **WHAT IS VISION? Proverb 28:19**
    a. Foresight with insight based on hindsight
    b. Seeing the invincible and making it visible
    c. An information bridge from the present to the future

d. The purpose of your existence
e. A God given idea
f. A clear-mental picture of a better future for your life
   "God's vision for your life is like a finger print: there is none exactly like it"

2. A LIFE WITHOUT VISION IS LIKE
* A purposeless, focusless, wandering personality
* Torchlight without batteries: willing but powerless
* A wedding without a bride: missing the essential element
* A car without Gas: capable of forward movement, but lacking necessary fuel
* A cow loose in pasture: just gazing

Without vision, there is nothing to strive for, no goal to pursue, no dream to realize and no success to attain.

3. THE NEED FOR VISION—John 3:25-31
* Your vision is your compass
* Your vision is your driving force
* Achievement is possible by vision
* Your vision motivates you
* Vision keeps you focused
* Vision helps you plan
* Vision is needed for evaluation

4. A MAN WITH A VISION
Everything we enjoy in life today is as a result of vision. No man can achieve great success without a clear-cut vision. In scripture, everyone that God called was given a vision to accomplish.

- When ALEXANDER THE GREAT had a vision, he conquered the then known world. When he lost his vision, he could not conquer the **liquor bottle**.
- When NOAH had a vision, he could resist the flood. When Noah lost his vision, he could not resist the **liquor bottle**.
- When SAMSON had a vision, he won many battles. When Samson lost his vision, he could not win the temptation **over his lust** for Delilah
- When SAUL had a vision, he conquered the kingdom. When Saul lost his vision, he could not conquer his own **jealousy**.
- When DAVID had a vision, he never lost a battle. When David lost his vision, he could not defeat his own **lust**.
- When AHAB had a vision, he conquered great nations. When Ahab lost his vision, he could not conquer his **sorrow and self-pity**.
- When SOLOMON had a vision, he was the wisest man in the world. When Solomon lost his vision, he could not control his own evil passions for **strange woman.**
- When ELIJAH had a vision, he prayed down fire from heaven and killed all the false prophets. When Elijah lost his vision, he ran from **one woman, Jezebel**, because he was afraid.
- When UZZIAH THE KING had a vision, he followed hard after God. When Uzziah lost his vision, he was ruined by the **greatness of his wealth**.
- When PETER had a vision, he was ready to die for Christ. When Peter lost his vision, he **denied his Lord**.
- When DEMAS had a vision, he was a fervent and effective minister of the gospel. When Demas lost his vision, **he went back** and became a judge that sentence Christians to their death.

REASONS FOR LOOSING GOD'S VISION
- Out-of-touch with God
- Burn out
- Impatience
- Absence of evaluation
- Egocentricity
- Seduced by other interest/visions.
- Life becomes tedious
- The vision becomes out dated

5. INGREDIENTS OF A WORTHWHILE VISION
a. It must be God-given and clearly defined
b. Received through God's leading
c. Time must be spent in prayer, fasting and working on your desire
d. Big enough to demand your wholehearted obedience
e. Positively affect the lives of others
f. Great enough to demand your total reliance upon God
g. Able to motivate you everyday.

6. HOW TO SECURE THE VISION FOR YOUR DESIRE
- State all your visions
- Examine all your motives
- Consider all your options
- Utilize all your resources
- Remove all your non essentials
- Embrace all your challenges.

Someone says, "When the goal-post is down, the game is over". It simply means that when there are no goals, there would be nothing to achieve. Your desire has to be accompanied by an achievable goal. When goal goes, desires goes. Setting goals is the practical step of bringing our desired vision into reality.

Without taking the practical step of setting goals, our visions would only remain on the drawing board.

Refusing to set goals is not a characteristic of spirituality. Many times we are unwilling to trust God to achieve the goals we outline for our desires. Many refuse to set goals as a result of ignorance, fear or failure and it has result in frustration.

1.   WHAT IS GOAL SETTING?
- Goals are decisions of attainment with a time frame
- Goal setting is the process of targeting growth over a specific period of time
- Goal setting is a statement of faith
- Goal setting provides the motivation, desire and effort to attain them.

2.   PRINCIPLES OF SETTING GOALS
- Achievable—they must be practical-
                I will graduate from college by . . . .
                I want to become president of the US
- Balanced in the sense that it must have the ability to bless others and accommodate them
- Concrete—definite, precise and concise
- Realistic—achievable within a time frame
- BIG—God must be pleased and glorify

Practical advice for goal setting

1.   Be sure to set reachable goals:
Goals that are unreachable discourage people and kill momentum. A missed goal is like a broken bone in the body—it takes a long time to heal. When you set an

unreachable goal and fail to achieve it, it demoralizes you and kills your desire

2. **Set SMART goals**
   Specific
   Measurable
   Attainable
   Reachable
   Timed

3. **Know your strength and weakness before setting goals**
   Don't copy any body to fulfill your desire, because their strength to endure some challenges might be different from yours. You have to ask yourself what you love doing, why you love doing them and what you need to get them done.

4. **Pray for God's guidance in setting your goals**
   a. Ask God for wisdom in setting your goals
   b. Pray about them until you are saturated
   c. Consider the problems and barriers to your desire before finally announcing it.
   d. When you finally make a decision by prayer then get up and make it work.

CHAPTER SIX

A Place Called There

This last part of this literature is vital; as it more specifically deals with 'how' to become the woman you desire to be. Certain requirements will be communicated in clear terms in this chapter. In the journey of life, often, there's a place called there, this refers to the promised land of our desires, the place of our dreams. However, it is only when you become who you should become that you will enjoy the pleasure of getting to the place of your dreams. The qualifications and prerequisites given here are vital actions we must learn, to make us into the right person for the crown we so much desire to wear. As it has been said earlier in this book, you must know the price, be ready to pay the price, but keep your eyes on the prize.

The price is what it will cost you to become the woman of your dreams, if you really want your dreams to come to pass, you cannot afford to keep sleeping. The prize is your promise land. You will get there in Jesus name. You will become the woman you desire to be. There's a place called THERE and you will get THERE.

Prerequisites For Becoming The Woman You Desire To Be

1. Be Determined To Create an Atmosphere Of Joy And Godliness Around Yourself.

Isaiah 12:3 KJV

"Therefore with joy shall ye draw water out of the wells of salvation?"

The help of God in the realization of our dreams requires an atmosphere of joy. In the school of faith, joy is a prerequisite. Resolute faith is identified by Godly peace. Godly peace is endorsed by a joyful and gladdened heart. Fear, gloom and sorrow are fore runners of evil and the devil, and such atmospheres drive away God's Sweet Spirit from operating. Without joy, you cannot draw water out of the well of salvation.

Isaiah 61:1-3 KJV

"The Spirit of the Lord God is upon me; because the Lord hath anointed me to preach good tidings unto the meek; he hath sent me to bind up the brokenhearted, to proclaim liberty to the captives, and the opening of the prison to them that are bound; [2] To proclaim the acceptable year of the Lord, and the day of vengeance of our God; to comfort all that mourn; [3] To appoint unto them that mourn in Zion, to give unto them beauty for ashes, the oil of joy for mourning, the garment of praise for the spirit of heaviness; that they might be called trees of righteousness, the planting of the Lord, that he might be glorified."

The Oil of joy must replace mourning and the garment of praise must replace the spirit of heaviness before God can be glorified in your situation. When the devil wins over your mood and takes your joy, he can confiscate your testimony. Every form of gloominess and crankiness must be dealt out of the way for The Holy Spirit of God to prevail over your situation and give you the desires of your heart. The other wing by which this bird flies is Godliness. Godliness will enhance your joyfulness and crown your life with unimaginable peace from God's throne.

Psalm 37:4 KJV

"Delight thyself also in the Lord; and he shall give thee the desires of thine heart."

With a Godly life, you're set up for delightful destiny.

Proverbs 10:24 KJV

"The fear of the wicked, it shall come upon him: but the desire of the righteous shall be granted."

The desires of the righteous shall be granted. In the school of victory, holiness is a prerequisite.

Obadiah 1:17 KJV

"But upon mount Zion shall be deliverance, and there shall be holiness; and the house of Jacob shall possess their possessions."

It is firmly essential for anyone whose desires must come to pass to be ready to create an atmosphere of joy and Godliness all around. This includes choosing your friends and acquaintances very carefully. An Eagle cannot afford to fraternize with Turkeys. Or else, she should bid the skies farewell and confine high flight to the dreams only.

1 Corinthians 15:33 KJV

"Be not deceived: evil communications corrupt good manners."

A major factor that determines your atmosphere are the friends you keep, the people you walk with, talk with and live with will definitely impact you positively or negatively. You must also be watchful of the things you hear and hearken unto, Who and what do you listen to or read?

Make sure you cultivate an enabling environment for your dreams to be actualized.

Ruth shut out bad influence by making Mama Naomi know that she's unstoppable:

Ruth 1:16-18 KJV

"And Ruth said, Intreat me not to leave thee, or to return from following after thee: for whither thou goest, I will go; and where thou lodgest, I will lodge: thy people shall be my people, and thy God my God: [17] Where thou diest, will I die, and there will I be buried: the Lord do so to me, and more also, if ought but death part thee and me. [18] When she saw that she was steadfastly minded to go with her, then she left speaking unto her.

The other sons of prophet told Prophet Elisa that his master would be taken from him today.

Look at his answer:

2 Kings 2:3 KJV

"And the sons of the prophets that were at Beth-el came forth to Elisha, and said unto him, Knowest thou that the Lord will take away thy master from thy head to day? And he said, Yea, I know it; hold ye your peace."

2 Kings 2:5 KJV

"And the sons of the prophets that were at Jericho came to Elisha, and said unto him, Knowest thou that the Lord will take away thy master from thy head to day? And he answered, Yea, I know it; hold ye your peace."

Look at the rendering in New Century Version:

2 Kings 2:3 NCV

The groups of prophets at Bethel came out to Elisha and said to him, "Do you know the Lord will take your master away from you today?" Elisha said, "Yes, I know, but don't talk about it."

2 Kings 2:5 NCV

The groups of prophets at Jericho came to Elisha and said, "Do you know that the Lord will take your master away from you today?" Elisha answered, "Yes, I know, but don't talk about it."

You must learn like the Prophet Elisa to shut negative influences out of your atmosphere. He told them to Shut their mouth up and not speak negative into his day. Creating an atmosphere of joy and godliness is a major step in your spiritual battle and winning the victory into your place of desire and destiny.

This first prerequisite leads and flows into the second one:

2. Don't Entertain Pity-Parties.

Ruth 1:11-15 KJV

"And Naomi said, Turn again, my daughters: why will ye go with me? are there yet any more sons in my womb, that they may be your husbands? [12] Turn again, my daughters, go your way; for I am too old to have an husband. If I should say, I have hope, if I should have a husband also to night, and should also bear sons; [13] Would ye tarry for them till they were grown? Would ye stay for them from having husbands? Nay, my daughters; for it grieveth me much for your sakes that the hand of the Lord is gone out against me. [14] And they lifted up their voice, and wept again: and Orpah kissed her mother in law; but Ruth clave unto her. [15] And she said, Behold, thy sister in law is gone back unto her people, and unto her gods: return thou after thy sister in law."

There are people around your dreams, who at certain times will make it their assignment to tell you why you can't become the woman you desire to be. They come as sympathizers, telling you how you're not the only one that will fail. Some even show empathy, giving you options and offering to help you lower your desires free of charge.

I silence anyone around your life, encouraging you to discourage your dreams. We never heard about Orpah all through the rest of the Bible, when you fall for the pity party, you end up in the pit.

You must be careful who you share your dreams with. When you share your 40 feet dream with a 2 feet individual, the only way he can understand it is to cut it to his own size. Bad things happen, when people laden with negative stories come to off load them upon your weary soul. Only sympathizers with the bucket and towel should be allowed, don't let anyone come and help lick your wounds. You need encouraging shoulders to cry on, not professional mourners that will turn your tears into wailing.

Instead of sinking in tears endlessly, encourage yourself and move forward.

Consider this story:

1 Samuel 30:1-8, 17-19 KJV

"And it came to pass, when David and his men were come to Ziklag on the third day, that the Amalekites had invaded the south, and Ziklag, and smitten Ziklag, and burned it with fire; [2] And had taken the women captives, that were therein: they slew not any, either great or small, but carried them away, and went on their way. [3] So David and his men came to the city, and, behold, it was burned with fire; and their wives, and their sons, and their daughters, were taken captive. [4] Then David and the people that were with him lifted up their voice and wept, until they had no more power to weep. [5] And David's two wives were taken captive, Ahinoam the Jezreelitess, and Abigail the wife of Nabal the Carmelite. [6] And David was greatly distressed; for the people spake of stoning him, because the soul of all the people was grieved, every man for his sons and for his daughters: but David encouraged himself in the Lord his God. [7] And David said to Abiathar the priest, Ahimelech's son, I pray thee, bring me hither the ephod. And Abiathar brought thither the ephod to David. [8] And David enquired at the Lord, saying, Shall I pursue after this troop? shall I overtake them? And he answered him, Pursue: for thou shalt surely overtake them, and without fail recover all. [17] And David smote them from the twilight even unto the evening of the next day: and there escaped not a man of them, save four hundred young men, which rode upon camels, and fled. [18] And David recovered all that the Amalekites had carried away: and David rescued his two wives. [19] And there was nothing lacking to them, neither small nor great, neither sons nor daughters, neither spoil, nor any thing that they had taken to them: David recovered all."

Pity parties drain your energy and destroy your strength.

3. Communicate Your Desires to Your Partner

There's no crime in asking for help and understanding.

It does not hurt to be helped by the ones you love.

Your spouse is your better half. A dream you cannot share with your husband portends danger. Danger for you, danger for your husband, danger for your relationship and danger for the dream or desire.

It is vital that you learn to concretely communicate your desires to your partner in a clear and precise manner. You both should live together in all its phases, your dreams must be cohesive and jointly crafted in love and Godly understanding.

No form of competitive actions must be allowed in your marriage.

Let's consider God's Word concerning the cohesion that is expected in your home and it's power:

1 Peter 3:7-8 KJV

"Likewise, ye husbands, dwell with them according to knowledge, giving honor unto the wife, as unto the weaker vessel, and as being heirs together of the grace of life; that your prayers be not hindered. [8] Finally, be ye all of one mind, having compassion one of another, love as brethren, be pitiful, be courteous"

Amos 3:3 KJV

"Can two walk together, except they be agreed?"

Ecclesiastes 4:8-12 KJV

"There is one alone, and there is not a second; yea, he hath neither child nor brother: yet is there no end of all his labor; neither is his eye satisfied with riches; neither saith he, For whom do I labor, and bereave my soul of good? This is also vanity, yea, it is a sore travail. [9] Two are better than one; because they have a good reward for their labor. [10] For if they fall, the one will lift up his fellow: but woe to him that is alone when he falleth; for he hath not another to help him up. [11] Again, if two lie together, then they have heat: but how can one be warm alone? [12] And if one prevail against him, two shall withstand him; and a threefold cord is not quickly broken."

These passages of The Holy Word of God are explicit pointers to the importance and power of sharing your desires with your partner. I also need to say that a shared ownership of your desires with your husband serves as a catalyst to fulfillment of such Godly desires.

Counsel for People in Difficult Marriages.

However, I must mention that if you are in a difficult or dysfunctional marriage, there's need for divine interference and God's intervention so that the man you're relating with will not be to you an enemy. This is a totally different matter that must be handled carefully. As much as I would love to deal with the handling of a difficult spouse, especially a difficult, unbelieving, demonized or dysfunctional husband, the scope of this book will not allow for a comprehensive approach. Yet I will give you the following counsels:

These counsels are actually meant for the children of God; therefore, if you have not given your life to Jesus Christ, accepting Him as your Lord and Savior by confessing and repenting from your sinful old ways, you will need to start from there. If I need to show you why, then the Bible passage below will help you out:

1 Peter 2:9-10 KJV

"But ye are a chosen generation, a royal priesthood, an holy nation, a peculiar people; that ye should shew forth the praises of him who hath called you out of darkness into his marvellous light: [10] Which in time past were not a people, but are now the people of God: which had not obtained mercy, but now have obtained mercy."

Certain promises of life are reserved for God's children, not every human being has the status of a child, some religions even believe that they are slaves, but Christians are Children of God and have access to an heritage that is only available to God's children.

Now that you're one of His own, we can proceed with the counsels:

a) Since there's nothing God cannot do, the first step, if you're already in a difficult marriage is to take matters to God in prayers. Commit your marriage, spouse and home into God's hands, inviting Him to intervene and heal, deliver and restructure everything that requires His touch.

(If you're still single, and you're fortunate to have this book in your hands, your first step is to become a true child of God, confess your sins and confess Jesus as your Lord and Savior, accepting Him into your life as your first and most important lover. This love life with Jesus will qualify you for the next important step which is to live a good and Godly life, one that pleases Christ and qualifies you to be married to another child of God like you. Then the third very important step here is to pray through for the will of God in choosing a marriage partner. If God is fully involved in the choosing process, you most likely will escape a problematic marriage. He gives His best to those who leave the choice to Him. The issues you might then have in marriage will not be for the emergency room.)

b) Learn everything you need to and that you can learn about a Christian marriage. Often, ignorantly living wrong could turn the people around us into enemies. A lot of times, the people closest to us are a mirror for us, pointing to who we are, serving as a reflection of the life that we live or they are products of our life style. They could be what we've pushed and made them to become by who we've been to them and in their lives.

Especially if your spouse was once a 'good' person but has now become a torn in the flesh for you, you might just need to trace back your steps to see what went wrong.

Learn all you can to become the right woman, wife and mother or partner to be loved, supported and cared for. Remember most good things are reciprocal. When you sow care you reap affection. Learn all about your husband's personality type and gender.

* I suppose a husband is a man and a wife is a woman. I do not intend to dabble into the homosexuality issue here, but think that naturally, the order I just mentioned above is as intended by God.

I believe that God's Word as seen below is very true:

Romans 1:26-28, 31-32 KJV

"For this cause God gave them up unto vile affections: for even their women did change the natural use into that which is against nature: [27] And likewise also the men, leaving the natural use of the woman, burned in their lust one toward another; men with men working that which is unseemly, and receiving in themselves that recompense of their error which was meet. [28] And even as they did not like to retain God in their knowledge, God gave them over to a reprobate mind, to do those things which are not convenient; [31] Without understanding, covenant breakers, without natural affection, implacable, unmerciful: [32] Who knowing the judgment of God, that they which commit such things are worthy of death, not only do the same, but have pleasure in them that do them."

Moreover, even animals have the males as daddy or husband and females as mummy or wife. It is as simple as ABC, even goats understand.

c) Once all is handed over to God and you have learned to become who you should be to your husband, God will work through your good heart, willingness to change and to fight for your marriage to kick the devil out of your home, but you will need this 3rd step. You need to wait patiently for God to perfect His work. Give God time to change things. Consider this scriptural instruction:

Hebrews 10:36 KJV

"For ye have need of patience, that, after ye have done the will of God, ye might receive the promise."

d) The final counsel I'm giving you on this matter is to have faith in God. Don't wander in unbelief. He'll come through for you.

Hebrews 10:35, 37-38 KJV

"Cast not away therefore your confidence, which hath great recompense of reward. [37] For yet a little while, and he that shall come will come, and will not tarry. [38] Now the just shall live by faith: but if any man draws back, my soul shall have no pleasure in him."

4. Build Your Empire (Home) With The Right Materials.

Proverbs 14:1 KJV

"Every wise woman buildeth her house: but the foolish plucketh it down with her hands."

Proverbs 9:1 KJV

"Wisdom hath built her house, she hath hewn out her seven pillars"

The seven pillars mentioned above are not a subject for the scope of this book, however, the woman, who really wants to become what she desires must build her home carefully with the help and wisdom of God. She needs to do so with the strong qualities of Patience, Love and Perseverance.

Patiently waiting on God and for God to make all things well in His own time.

Ecclesiastes 3:11 KJV

"He hath made everything beautiful in His time: also he hath set the world in their heart, so that no man can find out the work that God maketh from the beginning to the end."

Bishop David Oyedepo of The Living Faith Ministries said that: "If you appear before your time, you will disappear before your destiny."

Patience is a virtue of inner trust, restraint and strength to hold on to God's will and promises in the midst of eager expectations. It is the presence of inner control to delay immediate gratification and the capacity to be settled and orderly while waiting. Impatience is a major weakness that gives birth to bad temper and immature actions. It is coordinated by the spirit of error. I silence this evil spirit in your life today in Jesus name.

What impatience destroys in a moment would take repentance many years to repair if it is repairable.

Love when rightly channeled can overcome any opposition. It will disarm the deadliest of all antagonists.

Where love prevails life flourishes. True love engenders care and kindness.

Godly love for your spouse will rid all faults and imperfections of their weight.

1 Peter 4:8 AMP

"Above all things have intense and unfailing love for one another, for love covers a multitude of sins, forgives and disregards the offenses of others."

Proverbs 10:12 AMP

"Hatred stirs up contentions, but love covers all transgressions."

Love, when it is true moves us to act, sympathy could be deceptive, because it could be mockery in disguise, but true love is entangled in empathy.

1 John 3:18 KJV

"My little children let us not love in word, neither in tongue; but in deed and in truth."

Perseverance is patiently waiting and holding on to God and godliness in the face of opposition and maltreatment. Holding on against the tides and attacks of life. It is longsuffering, enduring ill-treatment and just hoping in God, even when one's loved ones are against her, causing her untold pain.

A woman who can be Patient, loving and persevering holds the right qualities and materials to build her own empire of peace, joy and fulfillment.

I need to mention that holding unto God in prayers and supplication, bundled with a strong faith in all the 3 building materials above is a very effective way of protecting your home from the enemy and the accuser of the brethren.

5. Shun Every Distraction.

It is pretty difficult to be focused and remain focused on the long run in the midst of so much daring distractions that populate our world and confront us on daily basis. Yet, shunning these distractions is an art to master if success is a must.

You cannot be who you desire to be if you follow after every passion, react to every action and allow yourself to be lured away in every direction possible. The key here is to know what you stand for so you will not fall for anything different or less. Jesus refused to be distracted by the pain of the cross because of the joy that was placed before Him. Joseph refused to be messed up by Portipha's wife because of his dreams and desires. Your desire is what pleases you, a sure pathway to it is to do what pleases your God. This was Joseph's formula for success.

Genesis 39:7-9 KJV

"And it came to pass after these things, that his master's wife cast her eyes upon Joseph; and she said, Lie with me. [8] But he refused, and said unto his master's wife, Behold, my master wotteth not what is with me in the house, and he hath committed all that he hath to my hand; [9] There is none greater in this house than I; neither hath he kept back anything from me but thee, because thou art his wife: how then can I do this great wickedness, and sin against God?"

". . . : HOW THEN CAN I DO THIS GREAT WICKEDNESS, AND SIN AGAINST GOD?"

Don't allow distractions tear your focus into pieces.

- A problematic loved one could be the distraction. Hand such over to God and let Him deal with him/her.
- Job and career difficulties could be it, keep your focus
- Peer pressure could be the distraction. Shun them.
- Ego and the attractions of sin could be it. Get the needed strength in the place of meditation on God's Word and prayer to conquer these as well.

Nothing should be strong enough to distract you from your goal and desire.

DISTRACTION IS NOTHING BUT EXCUSES!

*** Frances Jane Crosby (March 24, 1820-February 12, 1915), usually known as Fanny Crosby in the United States and by her married name, Frances van Alstyne, in the United Kingdom, was an American Methodist rescue mission worker, poet, lyricist, and composer. During her lifetime, she was well-known throughout the United States. By the end of the

19th century, she was "a household name "and "one of the most prominent figures in American evangelical life".

She became blind while an infant. Best known for her Protestant Christian hymns and gospel songs, Crosby was "the premier hymnist of the gospel song period", and one of the most prolific hymnists in history, writing over 8,000 hymns, with over 100 million copies of her songs printed.

Crosby was inducted into the Gospel Music Hall of Fame in 1975. Known as the "Queen of Gospel Song Writers "and as the "Mother of modern congregational singing in America" with "dozens of her hymns continuing to find a place in the hymnals of Protestant evangelicalism around the world" with most American hymnals containing her work, as "with the possible exception of Isaac Watts and Charles Wesley, Crosby has generally been represented by the largest number of hymns of any writer of the twentieth century in nonliturgical hymnals". Her gospel songs were "paradigmatic of all revival music" and Ira Sankey attributed the success of the Moody and Sankey evangelical campaigns largely to Crosby's hymns. Some of Crosby's best-known songs include "Blessed Assurance", "Pass Me Not, O Gentle Saviour", "Jesus Is Tenderly Calling You Home", "Praise Him, Praise Him", "Rescue the Perishing", and "To God Be the Glory".

Because some publishers were hesitant to have so many hymns by one person in their hymnals, Crosby used nearly 200 different pseudonyms during her career.

Crosby wrote over 1,000 secular poems and had four books of poetry published, as well as two best-selling autobiographies. Additionally, Crosby co-wrote popular secular songs, as well as political and patriotic songs, and at least five cantatas on biblical and patriotic themes, including The Flower Queen, the first secular cantata by an American composer. Crosby was committed to Christian rescue missions, and was known for her public speaking.

So, what's your distraction or excuse?

An illness, sickness, or mentality? Funny Crosby played the Guitar, Harp and Piano, ALTHOUGH BLIND FROM INFANTHOOD.

6. Don't Give Up In The Midst Of Challenges.

Only fickle minded women find another house, virtuous women fight for their home.

Your marriage and your dream are a twin worth fighting for. One of the most successful strategies of all time of the devil is to separate the woman from her marriage as price for her dreams and other successes. Many of the most famous women, who claim societal achievements today and in all history could not win at home. The woman God intended you to be is an all round winner. Not a looser at home, but a woman of strength.

Don't give up on your desires and don't ever give up on your marriage.

A wise man said: "Quitters don't win and winners don't quit." Don't adjust the theology of your life, desires and destiny to fit into the mould of your challenges. Don't reduce your expectations to the size of your experiences. Your experiences are in the passing, NO RETREAT NO SURRENDER.

Jesus had it tough in the garden of Gethsemane, but He did not give up.

When the going gets tough, the tough get going. If you ever have to die, make sure you do so 'climbing'. Don't die on the way down. Interestingly, all the children of God recorded in the scriptures who said:

"If we perish, we perish" never perished.
Ask Shedrach, Meshach and Abednego.
Ask Daniel.
And ask your Sister, Queen Esther.

Hebrews 10:38-39 KJV

"Now the just shall live by faith: but if any man draws back, my soul shall have no pleasure in him. [39] But we are not of them who draw back unto perdition; but of them that believe to the saving of the soul."

Hebrews 10:35 KJV

"Cast not away therefore your confidence, which hath great recompense of reward."

7.   Appreciate God For Where You Are.

Psalm 67:5-7 KJV

"Let the people praise thee, O God; let all the people praise thee. [6] Then shall the earth yield her increase; and God, even our own God, shall bless us. [7] God shall bless us; and all the ends of the earth shall fear him."

A major key to getting what you want from life is to be grateful to the giver of life Himself. As the governor among the nations, His generosity is all you need to become the woman you desire to be.

You may not be where you want to be right now, but you're not where you used to be. When you praise Him, be sure that He will raise you. The mystery of appreciating God is unfathomable. Behind an ungrateful heart is the operation of witchcraft. Ungrateful people cannot become great in life. Don't spend your life at the complaint counter, learn to praise God for where you are and for where He's taking you.

Conclusion

The Woman and Her Warfare

This is a vital issue I deliberately reserved for the end, like the best for the end. The battles of life are meant to make us better and not bitter. Check points are not stop points they are proof points. Road blocks are not dead ends, they are cautions in the journey of life. The road to becoming the woman you desire to be is a tough one, a warfare, but you have the promises and support of The One Who Never Fails. The El-Shaddai, All Sufficient and Breasted One. He will put everything at His disposal to fight for you. EVERYTHING AT HIS DISPOSAL MEANS EVERYTHING BECAUSE ALL THINGS ARE AT HIS DISPOSAL. EVERYTHING—INCLUDING YOUR ENEMIES.

Revelation 12:13-17 KJV

"And when the dragon saw that he was cast unto the earth, he persecuted the woman which brought forth the man child. [14] And to the woman were given two wings of a great eagle, that she might fly into the wilderness, into her place, where she is nourished for a time, and times, and half a time, from the face of the serpent. [15] And the serpent cast out of his mouth water as a flood after the woman, that he might cause her to be carried away of the flood. [16] And the earth helped the woman, and the earth opened her mouth, and swallowed up the flood which the dragon cast out of his mouth. [17] And the dragon was wroth with the woman, and went to make war with the remnant of her seed, which keep the commandments of God, and have the testimony of Jesus Christ."

The battle raging against you is beyond what you think, the support you have is also far beyond your wildest imagination.

The earth helped the woman. I see God using everything to fight for you.

You'll be helped beyond measure.

Just keep your relationship with The Master of the universe intact.

Let His Word not depart from your eyes, obeying Him in every step you take.

Let the fire of prayer never go down on the altar of your life, your marriage and your home.

Serve God with gladness, and rejoicing.

Worship Him with your whole being and life style.

You will see the goodness of The Lord in the land of the living.

I will see you at the top.

References

Baez, K. H. (2013). *Ruth*: Barbour Publishing Incorporated.

Bendroth, M. L. & Brereton, V. (2002). *Women and Twentieth-Century Protestantism*. Urbana: University of Illinois Press.

Brestin, D. (2012). *A Woman of Love*: David C Cook.

Childs, S. & Lena, M. (2010). *Women, Gender and Politics: A Reader*: Oxford University Press.

Daly, M. (1986). *The Church and the Second Sex With the Feminist Post Christian Introduction and New Archaic Afterwords, 3rd ed.* Boston: Beacon Press.

Drummond, L. A. (1996). *Women of Awakenings: The Historic Contribution of Women to Revival Movements*: Kregel Publications.

Elisabeth, S. F. (1994). *Searching the Scriptures*. New York: Crossroad.

Fausset, A. R. (1878). *"Definition for 'Moab' Fausset's Bible Dictionary"*: bible-history.com—Fausset.

Fiorenza, E. S. & Haering, H. (1999). *The nonordination of women and the politics of power*. Nijmegan, the Netherlands: Concilium.

Gench, F. T. (2004). *Back to the well: Women's encounters with Jesus in the Gospels*. Louisville, KY: Westminster

George, E. (2005). *The Remarkable Women of the Bible: And their Message for your Life Today:* Harvest House Publishers.

Griffith, R. M. (2000). *God's Daughters: Evangelical Women and the Power of Submission*: University of California Press.

Gross, R. (1996). *Feminism and religion*. Boston: Beacon Press.

James, J. W. (1980). *Women in American Religion*. Philadelphia: University of Pennsylvania Press.

Johnson, E. A. (2002). *The Church Women Want: Catholic Women in Dialogue*. New York: The Crossroad Publishing Company.

Johnson, M. S. (2005). *Women in Christianity*: Mittal Publications.

Juschka, D. (1999). *The category of gender in the study of religion*. Method & Theory in the Study of Religion.

Keener, C. S. (1992). *Paul, women, and wives: Marriage and women's ministry in the letters of Paul*. Peabody, MA: Hendrickson.

Kienzle, B. M., & Walker, P. J. (1998). *Women preachers and prophets through two millennia of Christianity*. Berkeley: University of California Press.

King, J. (1858). *Women*: Longley Publishers.

Lohman, R., & Sered, S. (2007). *Objects, gender, and religion*: Material Religion.

MacHaffie, B. J. (1992). *Readings in Her Story: Women in Christian Tradition*. Minneapolis, MN: Augsburg Fortress.

Malone, M. T. (2003). *Women and Christianity*. New York: Orbis Books.

Manning C. & Zuckerman P. (2005). *Sex and religion*. Belmont, CA: Wadsworth.

Mitch, S. (1999). *Courageous Love*: A Bible Study on Holiness for Women: Emmaus Road Publishing.

Nelson, T. (2005). *The 100 Most Important Bible Verses for Women*: Thomas Nelson Inc.

Rausch, T. P. (2003). *Catholicism in the Third Millennium*. Collegeville, MN: The Liturgical Press.

Rosser, S. V. & Johnson, D. G. (2006). *Women, Gender, And Technology*: University of Illinois Press.

Ruether, R. R. (2008). *Catholic Does Not Equal the Vatican.* New York: The New Press.

Wiersbe, W. W. (2010). The *Wiersbe Bible Study Series: Ruth/ Esther: Doing God's Will Whatever the Cost:* David C Cook.

World Council of Churches. (1998). *Eighth Assembly of the World Council of Churches:* Harare, Zimbabwe, December 3-14.

World Council of Churches. (2005). *Christian Perspectives on Theological Anthropology: A Faith and Order Study Document.* Faith and Order paper No. 199. Geneva: WCC Publications.

Young, P.D. (2004). *Women in Christianity.* In Leona M. Anderson, ed. and Pamela Dickey Young, eds., Women and Religious Traditions. New York: Oxford University Press.